CORE SKILLS

W9-AWS-535

Social Studies

ISBN-13: 978-1-4190-3424-4
ISBN-10:   1-4190-3424-3

Steck Vaughn™

A Harcourt Achieve Imprint

www.HarcourtSchoolSupply.com

Contents

Introduction

Social studies focuses on developing knowledge and skill in history, geography, culture, economics, civics, and government. It also focuses on people and their interaction with each other and the world in which they live. *Core Skills: Social Studies* addresses these areas of study and correlates with national social studies curriculum. With this book, students can:

- gain a better understanding of their community
- practice map and geography skills
- work with charts and other graphic devices

The book features 12 chapter lessons on a variety of social studies topics. It also includes:

- special features such as "Around the World" and "Special People"
- interactive questions about the text or pictures
- a unit project to expand student involvement with the topics
- chapter checkups
- unit tests

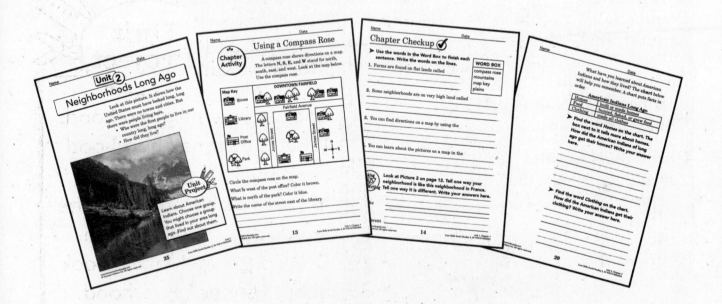

Core Skills Social Studies 2, SV 9781419034244

Unit 1

Neighborhoods Today

People live together in many different ways. You live with your family.

- Who lives next door?
- What is the place like where you live?

Unit Project

Look at your neighborhood. What is your neighborhood like? Think of some places in your neighborhood. Write words that describe them. Draw pictures. Make a book about your neighborhood.

CHAPTER 1
Neighborhoods Are for Living

The people who live near you are your **neighbors**. You are their neighbor. A **neighborhood** is a place where people live, work, and play.

This is a picture of Jenna's neighborhood.

➤ **Circle the places in Jenna's neighborhood that you have in your neighborhood.**

Find one thing neighbors are doing together. Write your answer here.

_____

- -

_____

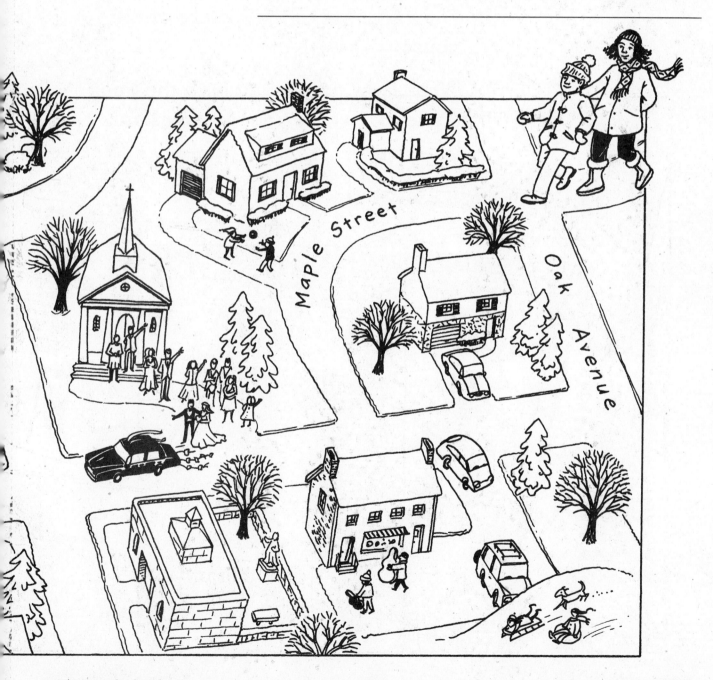

Jenna is going to draw a **map** of her neighborhood. A map is a drawing of a place. It shows whether things are close together or far apart. A map can also show what is to the left or right of something else.

Jenna is making a **map key**. The map key shows what the pictures on the map mean.

Here is part of Jenna's map key.

➤ **Put a ✔ next to the picture of the house.**

What does the picture with the book stand for? Write your answer here.

_____

- -

_____

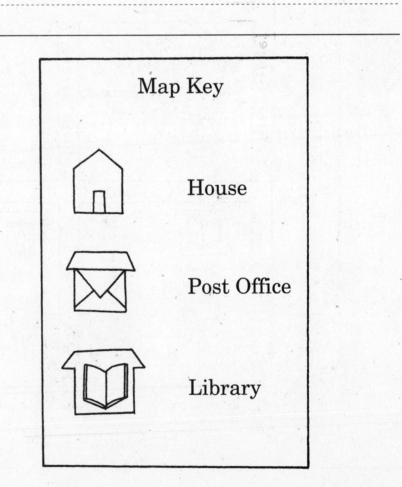

Map Key

House

Post Office

Library

This is Jenna's map of her neighborhood.

➤ **Circle the places where people live.**

Put a ✔ next to a place that is near the Art Museum.

A **compass rose** shows you which ways are north, south, east, and west. These ways are called **directions.** Find the compass rose.

➤ **What place is north of the library? Draw a line under the place.**

Jenna's Neighborhood

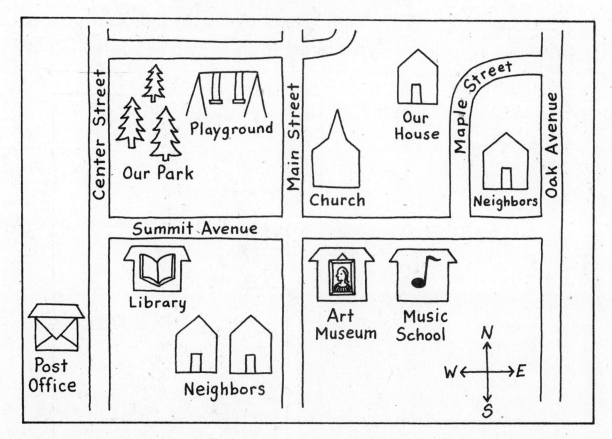

Mountain

Ocean

Neighborhoods are found in many different places. Some neighborhoods are in the **mountains**. A mountain is land that is very high. It is cold high up in the mountains. Sometimes there is snow at the top. People often ski in mountain neighborhoods.

Some neighborhoods are near **oceans**. An ocean is a large body of salt water. People may own boats and work to catch fish in ocean neighborhoods.

➤ **Look at the pictures. Put an X above the picture of a neighborhood in the mountains.**

What kinds of clothes would you wear if you lived high in the mountains? Why?

_____

_____

_____

_____

Plains

Rivers

Other neighborhoods are found on flat lands called **plains**. Many farms are found on the plains. This is because it is easier to farm on flat land than on hilly land.

You will also find neighborhoods near **rivers**. A river is a long stream of water that flows across land. Some rivers are so large that big ships can go on them.

➤ **Look at the pictures below. Circle the place you would most like to visit.**

Unit Project **Tip!**

Where is your neighborhood? Is it near mountains? Is it near the ocean? Is there a river nearby?

Where People Live

People live in neighborhoods all around the world. These neighborhoods may be near oceans. Or they may be in the mountains. One thing is the same about all of them. All neighborhoods have places for people to live, work, and play.

Look at these pictures. They show neighborhoods in countries far away. Picture 1 shows a neighborhood in England. Picture 2 shows a neighborhood in France.

➤ **How are these neighborhoods alike? Write your answer here.**

_____

_____

_____

_____

Chapter Activity

Using a Compass Rose

A compass rose shows directions on a map. The letters **N, S, E,** and **W** stand for north, south, east, and west. Look at the map below. Use the compass rose.

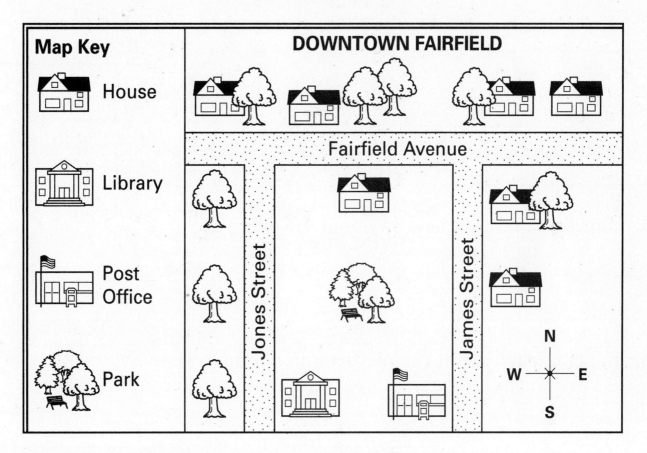

1. Circle the compass rose on the map.

2. What is west of the post office? Color it brown.

3. What is north of the park? Color it blue.

4. Write the name of the street east of the library.

_____

- -

Chapter Checkup ✓

➤ **Use the words in the Word Box to finish each sentence. Write the words on the lines.**

WORD BOX

compass rose
mountains
map key
plains

1. Farms are found on flat lands called

_____

_____ .

2. Some neighborhoods are on very high land called

_____

_____ .

3. You can find directions on a map by using the

_____

_____ .

4. You can learn about the pictures on a map in the

_____

_____ .

Thinking & Writing

Look at Picture 2 on page 12. Tell one way your neighborhood is like this neighborhood in France. Tell one way it is different. Write your answers here.

_____

Like _____

_____

Different _____

Talk with your friends or family about your neighborhood. Answer these questions.

- **What is your neighborhood like?**

- **What are some of the places in your neighborhood?**

- **What rivers, ocean, or mountains are near your neighborhood?**

Now decide how you will present your project. Try one of these ideas or think of another one.

- Make your book. Use words and sentences to tell about your neighborhood. Use your pictures in your book.

- Draw a map of your neighborhood. Show streets and the places where people live, work, and play. Draw a compass rose. Draw a map key.

Unit 1 ✎ Test

➤ **Read each sentence. Write T on the line if the sentence is true. Write F if it is false.**

_____ 1. People do not work in neighborhoods.

_____ 2. A compass rose shows the directions on a map.

_____ 3. A map key tells what pictures on a map mean.

_____ 4. Some neighborhoods are found on the plains.

_____ 5. Neighborhoods always stay the same.

Thinking & Writing

How might you use a map of your neighborhood? Tell one way. Write your answer here.

_____

_____

_____

_____

CHAPTER 5

People Give Us Goods and Services

Needs are things people must have to live. Food, clothes, and a place to live are three needs that all people have.

Wants are things people would like to have. Toys, trips, and pets are some of the things people want.

The children in one class want different things. Look at the picture graph. A **picture graph** uses pictures to show facts. This picture graph shows how many children want each thing.

➤ **Five children want a ball. Color the 5 balls on the graph.**

Three children want a kite. Draw 3 kites on line 2.

One child wants a hat. Draw 1 hat on line 3.

What we want	How many?
1. ball	◯ ◯ ◯ ◯ ◯
2. kite	
3. hat	

Many people work in your **community**. A community is a town or city where people live, work, and play. There are many neighborhoods in one community. Your neighbors work to make the things you need and want. These things are called **goods**.

Goods are made in a factory. Many toys are made in a factory. So are clothes. These things are goods.

People have different jobs in a factory. Look at the pictures. These people work with machines. The machines help the workers do their jobs. What does each worker do?

➤ **Which worker sews clothes? Put a <u>C</u> over the picture.**

Which worker makes bottles? Put a <u>B</u> over the picture.

Sometimes many people work together to make goods. Look at the picture below. An automobile is so big that it takes many people to make it. Each person does a different job.

Sometimes people make different parts of a good. Then the parts are sent to one place to be put together.

People often use machines to make goods. The machines make the work easier. Machines also help workers do their jobs faster.

➤ **Look at the picture. What machines are the workers using to make the cars? Circle the machines.**

Some people in the community work to help us. They give us **services**. A service is a job someone does to help other people. People who work in service jobs do not make goods.

Your community has workers who give services. There are workers who keep the neighborhoods clean. Firefighters put out fires. Police officers work to keep your neighborhood safe. Doctors and nurses care for people who are sick. Your community has these services to help make your neighborhood better.

➤ **Look at the pictures. They show some community workers. What do these people do? Write your answer under each picture.**

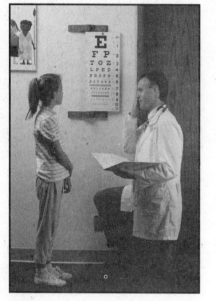

1. _____

_____

_____

2. _____

_____

_____

Many businesses give services, too. People work together at service businesses to help others. A restaurant is a service business. People there cook and serve food. A television station is also a service business. The news is one service a television station gives. Many people work together to bring news to people all over the United States.

➤ **What workers have given you a service? Write the names of two jobs here.**

1. _____

2. _____

Unit Project **Tip!**

What kinds of jobs do adults you know have? Ask them what they do at their jobs. Do most of the jobs give services or make goods? List the jobs.

Technology

How We Get Goods

How do goods get to the people who need them? Many things we need or want are made far from where we live.

Many goods are sent from place to place on trains and trucks. Some goods, like milk, must be kept cold. Milk is moved in a special kind of truck.

There are special train cars to move goods, too. There are train cars for moving heavy goods, like tractors. Other train cars are built to carry food, like corn.

 Do you think ice cream is moved in a special truck? Why? Write your answer here.

_____

_____

_____

_____

Goods from Far Away

Some goods we need and want come from other countries. We need people in other countries to make or grow these goods for us.

We do not grow all the food we eat in the United States. Some food is grown in other countries. For instance, some bananas we eat come from Brazil. Brazil is a country on the continent of South America.

Some of the rubber we use comes from Sri Lanka. Sri Lanka is in Asia. Rubber trees grow there. People work in rubber tree forests to get the rubber. It is made into many goods that we use.

➤ **Do you use goods made of rubber? Does your family? Make a list. Write your list here.**

_____

_____

_____

_____

_____

Working with a Picture Graph

A **picture graph** uses pictures to show facts. This picture graph shows the **community workers** in Job City. These workers give **services.**

Job City Community Workers

Kind of Worker	Number of Workers
Firefighter	🪖 🪖 🪖 🪖 🪖 🪖 🪖
Mail Carrier	
School Crossing Guard	🛑 🛑 🛑 🛑

1. Circle the title of the graph.

2. How many crossing guards work in Job City?

_____

- -

_____

3. How many firefighters are there?

_____

- -

_____

4. Five mail carriers work at the post office. Draw a stamp on the graph for each of them.

Chapter Checkup ✓

➤ **Read each sentence. Find the word in the Word Box to finish each sentence. Write the word on the line.**

WORD BOX
needs
service
community
goods

1. A town or city with many neighborhoods is a

_____

_____ .

2. Food, clothes, and a place to live are

_____

_____ .

3. The things people make to meet our needs and wants are

_____

_____ .

4. The post office worker gives us a

_____

_____ .

Thinking & Writing **Look at the workers in the pictures. Do they give us goods, or do they give us services? Write your answer here.**

_____

_____

_____

CHAPTER 6 Why People Work

How do people choose what kinds of jobs they have? Sometimes people do what they really like. Teachers like working with children and helping them learn. A baseball player really likes to play baseball. These people enjoy doing their jobs.

➤ **Think about what you like to do. What kind of job would you like? Write your answer here.**

_____

- -

_____

Draw a picture of yourself doing the job you like. Draw your picture in the box below.

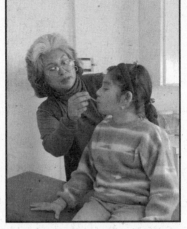

Some people choose a job because they want to help others. These people care for us when we are sick. They keep us safe. We need people to do these jobs.

➤ **Think about your town. What is one job that must be done every day? Who does it? Write your answer here.**

_____

_____

_____

_____

_____

_____

_____

Unit Project

✂ **Tip!**

Think of jobs in your community. Ask some workers why they work. Why did they choose their jobs?

Sometimes people have special jobs because of where they live. Many people in the neighborhood may have the same kinds of jobs.

People living near water may fish or work on a boat. Other people have jobs fixing boats. Still other people sell things needed for fishing.

Think about other places that people live. What kinds of jobs do people have on the plains? What kinds of jobs do people have in the mountains?

➤ **Look at picture 1. This worker lives and works near the water. Circle his job.**

fixing boats

painting

unloading fish

➤ **Look at picture 2. This worker lives in the mountains. There is a lot of snow in the mountains. Circle his job.**

teaching

moving snow

farming

Who is working in the picture above? The teacher and the children are working. Think of all the jobs students do in school. Their most important job is to learn. But they have other jobs, too. Keeping the classroom clean is one job.

➤ **Look at the picture. Circle each person who is working.**

What kinds of jobs are done at your home? Someone has to cook and clean. Someone has to wash the clothes. What kinds of jobs do you have at home?

➤ **Name one job you have at home. Write your answer here.**

_____

- -

_____

Harriet Tubman

Most people are paid to work. Sometimes people will work without pay. These people are **volunteers**. Volunteers choose to work for free. A **slave** is someone who is *forced* to work without pay. Slaves are not free. They cannot choose where to work or live. Long ago, some people in the United States were slaves.

Harriet Tubman was a woman who helped slaves escape to freedom. Harriet Tubman was born a slave in the state of Maryland. She escaped from slavery when she was 30 years old. Later she went back to Maryland. She wanted to help other slaves become free. She went back to Maryland 19 times. Each time she led more slaves to freedom. In all, she helped 300 slaves escape.

➤ **What job would you like to do to help people? Write your answer here.**

_____

_____

_____

_____

_____

_____

Working with a Chart

Look at the chart. It shows jobs done by workers. Some workers listed on the chart give us goods. Others give us services.

The first worker on the chart is a police officer. There is a ✔ under the word *Services*. A police officer gives us services. Read the names of the other workers on the chart. Put a ✔ under the word *Goods* if the worker gives us goods. Put a ✔ under the word *Services* if the worker gives us services.

Worker	Goods	Services
Police Officer		✔
Teacher		
Farmer		
Dentist		
Worker in a shoe factory		
Baker		

Chapter Checkup ✔

➤ **Read each sentence. Write T on the line if the sentence is true. Write F if it is false.**

_____ 1. No one likes to work.

_____ 2. Some people choose a job because they want to help others.

_____ 3. Some people have special jobs because of where they live.

_____ 4. You have many jobs during the school day.

Name a job you would like to do to make your neighborhood a better place to live. Tell why you want to do that job. Write your answer here.

_____

_____

_____

_____

CHAPTER 7 Where Does the Money Go?

The goods and services people need and want cost money. People must work to make money. The money people get for doing a job is called their **income**.

Most people do not have enough money to buy all they need and want. They must choose how to spend their income. They think about what they need and want most. Then they think about how much money they have.

➤ **How are these people spending their income? Draw an <u>N</u> on the person buying something that is a need.**

Draw a <u>W</u> on the person buying something that is a want.

Many people use a **budget** to help them spend their money. A budget is a plan for how to spend money. A budget helps you know how much money you have and how much you can spend.

This family wants to go on a trip. They are making a budget. Put an **X** next to each question about a budget that they must answer.

_____

_____ How much will the trip cost?

_____ How much income do we have?

_____ Where should we go?

_____ What clothes shall we take?

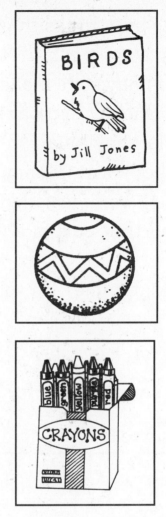

When people make a budget, they list their needs first. Then they write down how much the goods and services they need will cost. Finally, they write down their income. The budget will show how much income will be left after paying for their needs.

Money that is left can be spent on goods and services people want. They cannot buy all they want. So they must choose those things they want the most.

➤ **Pretend that after buying your needs, you have $5.00 left to buy wants. Look at the list.**

WANTS

Book $4.00	Game $6.00
Crayons $2.00	Ball $1.00
Puzzle $3.00	

Which wants can you buy? Write your answer here.

_____

- -

_____

Unit Project **Tip!**

Remember that a volunteer is a person who chooses to work without pay. Think about your community. What kinds of volunteer jobs can children do? Ask about other kinds of volunteer jobs in your community. Make a list of volunteer jobs in your community.

Sometimes people want to buy things that cost a lot of money. They may want a car, a bicycle, or a television. People may save money to buy these things. They put money in a bank a little at a time. After a while, they have enough money to buy what they want. Money that is put in a safe place like a bank is called **savings**. Savings are an important part of a budget.

Do you have a piggy bank at home? Do you put money in it every week? If you do, then you have some savings, too.

➤ **What would you like to save money for? Draw a picture of it here.**

Communities give services to the people who live in them. Police officers and other workers give these services. The communities must pay these workers. People give money to the community where they live. The money people pay to the community is called **taxes**.

 Look at the pictures. The community pays these people with tax money. How does each person help you? Write your answer next to the picture.

Teacher

Police Officer

Librarian

Communities need tax money for other things, too. Look at the picture above. It shows roads and bridges. Tax money is used to build roads and bridges like these. Taxes also pay to have the roads fixed.

Sometimes the community library needs new books. Tax money is used to buy the books. Taxes are used to build new schools or to fix up old ones. Taxes are used for all these things and more. Taxes help make your community a better place to live.

➤ **Think about your community. What would happen if no one fixed a big hole in the street? Write your answer here.**

_____

- -

_____

_____

- -

_____

www.harcourtschoolsupply.com
66
Unit 3, Chapter 7
Core Skills Social Studies 2, SV 9781419034244

Name _____ Date _____

Technology

Making Money

All our money is made in factories owned by the government. Coins are one kind of money. First, big sheets of metal are cut into circles. Then the circles are heated. The words and pictures are pressed into them.

Paper money is printed on large sheets of paper. Each sheet has 32 bills printed on it. The bills are then cut apart.

Coins and paper money show the dates they were made. They also have pictures of famous Americans on them. When new money is made, an artist makes a drawing. Then the picture is engraved, or carved, onto a steel plate.

➤ **Pretend the government is paying you to make a new bill. What would you show on it? Draw your new bill here.**

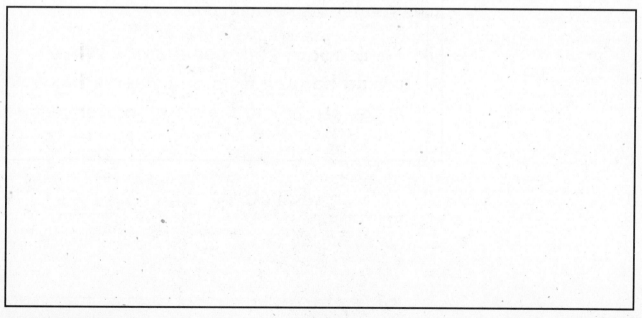

Core Skills Social Studies 2, SV 9781419034244

Working with a List

Chapter Activity

Look at the words in the box below. Some name *needs*. Some name *wants*. Look at the list below the box. Write the names of needs under the word *Needs*. Write the names of wants under the word *Wants*. The list has been started for you.

candy bar	**bowl of soup**	**house**
water	**balloon**	**coat**
TV	**shoes**	**computer**

Needs
water

Wants
candy bar

Completing a Chart

Complete a chart that tells about paper money. Look at the chart below. Some facts are missing from the chart. Now look at the list of facts. Use the facts to finish the chart.

Facts

George Washington's face is on the $1 bill.
Abraham Lincoln's face is on the $5 bill.
Alexander Hamilton's face is on the $10 bill.
Andrew Jackson's face is on the $20 bill.

Paper Money

Name of Bill	Important Person Pictured
	George Washington
$5	Abraham Lincoln
	Alexander Hamilton
$20	

Chapter Checkup ✓

➤ **Read each question. Circle the correct answer.**

1. Why do people make budgets?

   to help them choose services they want

   to help them plan how to spend their money

   to help them earn money

2. What is one reason we need savings?

   to buy things we want that cost a lot of money

   to buy food

   to pay for community services

3. How do communities pay for the services they give people who live in them?

   They use someone's income.

   They do not pay for services.

   They use the money they get from taxes.

What would happen if people did not pay taxes? Tell two things. Write your answer here.

_____

_____

_____

_____

_____

Name _____ Date _____

Using a Picture Graph

The picture graph shows how many people give services to a community. Look at the picture graph. Then answer the questions.

Kinds of Service Workers	How Many?
Judges	🔨 🔨 🔨 🔨 🔨 🔨
School bus drivers	🚌 🚌 🚌 🚌
City park workers	

1. How many judges work for the community?

_____

_____

2. How many school bus drivers are there?

_____

_____

3. The community also pays 6 city park workers. Draw a tree on the graph for each worker.

4. Name 2 things in your community that you could tell about on a picture graph.

_____

_____

_____

_____

Present Your Project

Now it's time to finish your project. Think about what you learned about workers. Answer these questions.

- **What kinds of work do people you know do?**

- **What kinds of jobs do people in your community have?**

- **What can volunteer workers do?**

- **What kind of volunteer work can children do?**

Now decide how you will present your project. Try one of these ideas or think of another one.

- Write a story about someone who has a job you learned about. Tell what the person does at work. Is the person a volunteer or a service worker, or does the person make goods?

- Draw some pictures of workers showing what each worker does.

- Make a poster of jobs people do. Show on the poster if the workers are service workers, volunteers, or workers who make goods.

Unit 3 🖉 Test

➤ **Read each sentence. Find the word in the Word Box to finish each sentence. Write the word on the line.**

WORD BOX

wants
services
slaves
income

1. Money that people are paid for working is

_____

- -

_____ .

2. Toys, pets, and piano lessons are

_____

- -

_____ .

3. People who could not live or work where they wanted were

_____

- -

_____ .

4. Some people work to help other people. These workers give

_____

- -

_____ .

Thinking & Writing **What does your community spend tax money on? Name two things. Write your answers here.**

_____

- -

_____

_____

- -

_____

Unit 4

People Make Rules and Laws

People of all ages live, work, and play together in neighborhoods.

- How do people get along with each other?
- How do people work together to fix problems?

Unit Project

Think about a problem in your community. Make a rule that would make your community better for everyone. Do this as you read Unit 4.

CHAPTER 8 Rules and Laws for Everyone

People make **rules**. Rules tell us what to do or what not to do. They help us work and play together.

Rules are important. Some rules keep us safe. Other rules keep the places we live in or work in safe. Still other rules keep things fair.

These children are in their school cafeteria. What rules are they following? How do the rules help them work and play together?

➤ **What is one rule you follow during the school day? Write your answer here.**

_____

- -

_____

Look at the pictures. They show rules you may have in your neighborhood. What rules do these pictures tell about?

➤ **Draw a line from the rule to the correct picture.**

Wait your turn in line without fooling around.

Each player gets a turn at bat.

➤ **Why is it important for everyone to follow rules? Write your answer here.**

_____

- -

_____

- -

_____

Laws are rules for communities. They help people live together. Laws are written down so everyone knows what they are. Laws help keep the community safe and clean. They help keep things fair.

Look at the pictures of the traffic signs. Find the stop sign. The stop sign tells drivers to stop. Stopping for a stop sign is one law you have in your community. This law helps keep the community safe for everyone.

➤ **What does the speed limit sign tell car drivers? Write your answer here.**

_____

- -

_____

 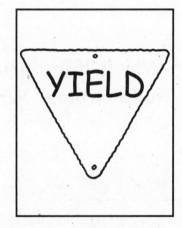 

➤ **Think about laws in your community. What is one law you must follow? Write your answer here.**

_____

- -

_____

➤ **Match each law below with the correct picture. Write the number of the law in the box next to the picture.**

1. Obey all traffic laws.

2. Walk your dog on a leash.

3. Throw litter in the litter basket.

➤ **Put a ✔ next to the picture that shows someone who is not obeying the law.**

Unit Project

Tip!

Think of a problem in your community. How could the problem be fixed? Write down all your ideas.

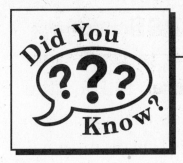

Signs Help You

Signs tell you about rules and laws. The signs in your neighborhood help you remember the laws where you live. Some signs use words. Some signs just use pictures to help you remember rules or laws. Some signs even have lights to help you see them.

Look at these signs. Do you have them in your neighborhood? What do they tell you?

➤ **Your neighborhood has rules.**

Make a sign that shows one rule. Draw your sign here.

Matching Pictures

Your community uses signs to tell you the rules. Many signs tell the rules with pictures. Look at the rules and pictures. Draw a line from each picture to the rule it matches.

No Bicycles

Walk

Don't Walk

No Right Turn

No Dogs

Chapter Checkup ✓

➤ Read each question. Circle the correct answer.

1. Why do people make rules and laws?

   Rules and laws cause problems.

   Everyone likes rules and laws.

   Rules and laws help people live together.

2. What rule is this boy breaking?

   Obey all traffic laws.

   Walk your dog on a leash.

   Don't litter.

3. Why does this neighborhood need a law about riding bicycles?

   to keep children from having fun

   to keep people safe

   to keep things fair

Name one rule or law you obeyed today. Tell how it helps people live together. Write your answer here.

_____

_____

_____

_____

CHAPTER 9 — Leaders and Laws

How are new laws made? How are old laws changed? Look at the picture below. These people are talking about a law in their community. They want to change the law.

The people talk to their community **leaders**. A leader is a person who leads or is in charge. Community leaders make up the **government**. The government is those people who make the laws and see that the laws are obeyed.

➤ **What law would you like to change? Write your answer here.**

_____

- -

_____

Who are the community leaders? Communities have many leaders. Some communities have a **mayor**. The mayor is an important leader. The mayor works to keep the community a good place to live.

The people of a community choose their leaders. Each person gets to **vote** for, or pick, one person for each job. Then all the votes are counted. The person with the most votes is the leader.

➤ **Who is the leader of your community? What would you like to ask this person? Write your answer here.**

_____

_____

_____

Unit Project **Tip!**

Talk to other children and adults. Tell them your ideas for fixing the problem. Ask them if they have other ideas for fixing the problem. Make a list.

Your community is in a **state**. There are 50 states in the United States. Look at the map of the United States.

Look at the two boxes on the map that show Alaska and Hawaii. These are two of the states. They are far away from the other states. On most maps of the United States, they are shown in boxes like these. These boxes are called **insets**.

▶ **Look at the map of the United States. Find your state and circle the name.**

Underline the names of the states that are next to your state.

Each state has a leader called the **governor**. The governor works to keep people in the state safe. The governor tries to make sure everyone is treated fairly.

The leader of the United States is the **President**. People in the United States vote to choose the President.

Government Leaders	
City or Town	Mayor
State	Governor
United States	President

➤ **What is the name of your state's governor? Write your answer here.**

_____

- -

_____

What is the name of the President of the United States? Write your answer here.

_____

- -

_____

Who leads your town? Is it a mayor? Write the name of your town's leader here.

_____

- -

_____

The **capital** is the city where the government meets. The governor and other state leaders work in the state capital.

The President works in the capital of the United States. The name of the capital of the United States is Washington, D.C. Leaders from all the states meet here. They make the laws for our country.

➤ **What is the name of the capital of your state?**

_____

- -

_____

Special People

Frederick Douglass

Long ago, much of the work on big farms was done by slaves. These slaves could not go to school or choose their jobs. The law said they were slaves. Frederick Douglass did not think this was fair. He spent his life working to change this law.

Frederick Douglass talked to President Lincoln about the slaves. He wrote in books and newspapers about the unfair law. Finally, the law was changed. Slavery ended. Today, there are no slaves in the United States because Douglass helped get the law changed.

➤ **What can you do to change an unfair rule or law? How can you get it changed? Write your answer here.**

_____

_____

_____

_____

Chapter Activity

Reading a Map of North America

Look at the map of North America. It shows three countries on the continent of North America. Each has a capital. Use the compass rose.

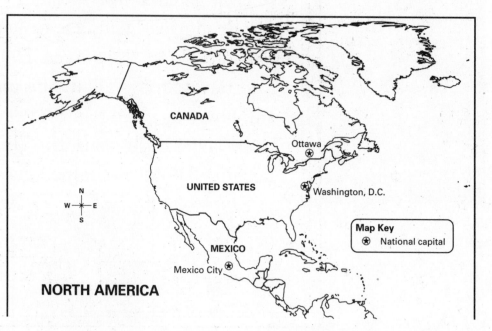

1. **Find the country north of the United States. Color the country to the north green.**

2. **Circle the three capitals on the map.**

3. **Write the name of the capital of the United States.**

_____

- -

_____

4. **Find the country south of the United States. Color the country to the south brown.**

Unit 4, Chapter 9
Core Skills Social Studies 2, SV 9781419034244

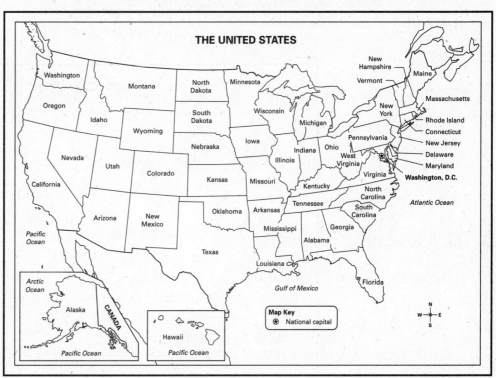

Chapter Activity

Finding Places in the United States

Look at the map of the United States. Remember to use the compass rose.

1. What does the ✪ on the map key mean?

_____

- -

_____

2. Draw an **X** on your state. Draw an **O** on a state north or south of your state.

3. Which direction is Ohio from Indiana?

_____

- -

_____

Chapter Checkup ✓

▶ **Finish each sentence. Circle the correct answer.**

1. People who make the rules for a community are the

   teachers   leaders   children

2. People in a community choose their own leaders.
   Each person gets to

   vote   rule   mayor

3. The leader of a state is the

   mayor   President   governor

4. The leader of the United States is the

   mayor   President   governor

Thinking & Writing

**Why is it important to have good leaders?
Write your answer here.**

_____

- -

_____

- -

_____

CHAPTER 10 People Solve Problems Together

Sometimes people have a problem. They can try to fix it by working together.

Mr. Turner works at night. He sleeps during the day. After school, children play next to Mr. Turner's house. They make a lot of noise. The noise keeps Mr. Turner awake. He wants the children to stop playing near his house.

➤ **What can Mr. Turner do about the problem? Write your answer here.**

_____

_____

_____

Mr. Turner talks with the children and their parents. The children do not have another place to play. What can they do?

Then they have an idea. There is a small field near Mr. Turner's house. No one uses the field. The grass is tall. Old cans, papers, and other trash are everywhere. The children and their parents and Mr. Turner talk. They decide to work together to clean up the field.

➤ **What needs to be done? Write your answer here.**

_____

_____

_____

On Mr. Turner's day off, everyone begins to work. It is hard work. It takes many days to finish the job. But now the children have a place to play. Mr. Turner can sleep.

➤ **Look at the picture. How are people helping? Circle each thing they are doing.**

digging

picking up cans and paper

washing the fence

raking the grass

The community leaders made the field into a community park. They put up signs where the children play. The signs remind people not to throw trash on the ground. Everyone helps keep the new park clean. It belongs to all of them.

Mr. Turner and his neighbors worked together to fix their problem. They also made their neighborhood a nicer place to live.

➤ **Think about your community. Can you make it a nicer place to live? Draw a picture of what you can do.**

Unit Project **Tip!**

List all the ideas you have to fix the problem in your community. Together pick the three best ways. Use these ways to make a rule that could help fix the problem.

www.harcourtschoolsupply.com
94   Unit 4, Chapter 10
Core Skills Social Studies 2, SV 9781419034244

Mr. Turner and his neighbors worked to clean up a field. Sometimes cleaning up a community is a bigger job. The air, water, and land can get dirty. This is called **pollution**.

Pollution often covers a large area. Dirty air may blow from one state to another. A dirty river in your town may be dirty in other communities. These are big problems. Often, people in many communities must work together to clean up pollution.

Look at the picture. Pretend this place is in your community. How could your community make the air cleaner? Talk with your friends and family about what you could do.

World Wildlife Fund

Sometimes people all around the world share a problem. They work together to fix it. One group that does this is the World Wildlife Fund. This group works to keep animals and the places they live safe.

The World Wildlife Fund is helping save tigers in Asia and elephants in Africa. It is working to save other animals around the world. The World Wildlife Fund is working to save rain forests and to keep the oceans clean.

➤ **Make a poster for the World Wildlife Fund.**

Remind people to work together to protect our world and the animals living in it.

Tiger

Mountain Gorilla

Chapter Activity

Using a Map of the World

This world map shows where some animals live. These animals are in danger. Groups like the World Wildlife Fund want to keep these animals safe.

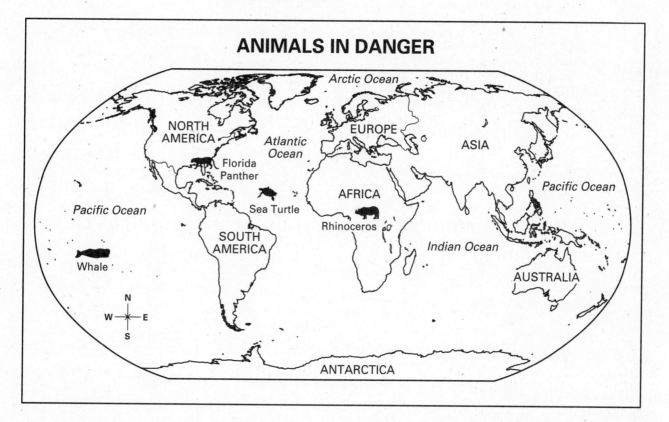

ANIMALS IN DANGER

_____

- -

1. What animal in danger lives in Florida? _____

2. What two animals live in oceans? Circle their names below.

   rhinoceros   Florida panther   whale   sea turtle

3. Tigers live in Asia. Put a **T** on the map where tigers live.

4. Grizzly bears live in North America. Put a **B** where they live.

Chapter Checkup ✓

➤ **Read each sentence. Write T on the line if the sentence is true. Write F if it is false.**

_____

_____ **1.** Problems can be fixed only by making new laws.

_____ **2.** People in a community can work together to fix their problems.

_____ **3.** Community leaders put up signs that tell us rules and laws.

_____ **4.** If the community cannot find an answer to a problem, there is no one else to help.

Thinking & Writing **How could you stop people from throwing trash on the ground in your community? Think of two things you could do. Write your answers here.**

_____

_____

_____

_____

Name _____   Date _____

Reading a Map of the United States

Look at this map of the United States. Read each sentence. Do what it tells you to do.

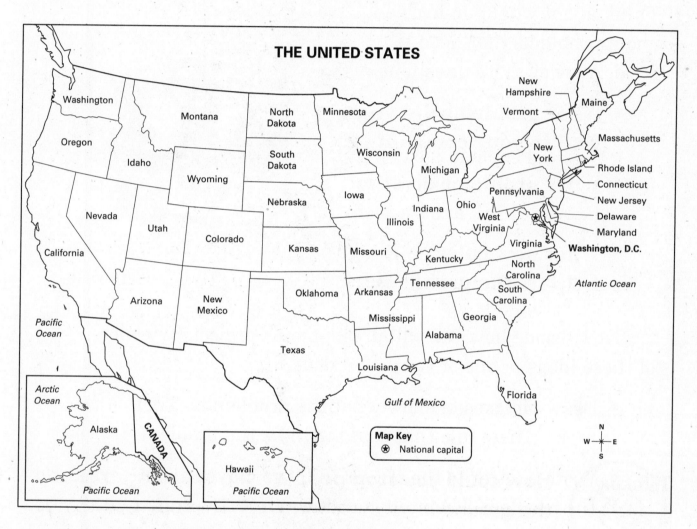

THE UNITED STATES

1. Circle the capital of the United States.

2. Color three states on the East coast red.

3. Color three states next to the Pacific Ocean blue.

4. Write an **N** on the north part of Alaska.

Present Your Project

Now it's time to finish your project. Think about what you learned about problems that need to be fixed. Answer these questions.

RULES
1. Work quietly.
2. Share materials.
3. Stay in your center.
4. Help others.

- **What problems did you find in your community?**

- **What problems do other people think are important?**

- **What new rules could help fix the problems?**

Now decide how you will present your project. Try one of these ideas or one of your own ideas.

- Draw pictures to show what the problem is. Then make a new rule that could help fix the problem.

- Write a letter to the mayor. Tell the mayor about the problem. Then tell your idea for a new rule to fix the problem. Sign your name to the letter.

- Act out the problem you have worked on. Then act out what things would be like if there was a rule that fixed the problem.

Unit 4 ✏ Test

➤ **Read each sentence. Find the word in the Word Box to finish each sentence. Write the words on the lines.**

WORD BOX

laws

governor

vote

pollution

_____

1. In the United States, people _____ for new leaders.

2. In our communities, _____ help keep us safe.

3. Dirty air is one kind of _____.

4. The _____ is the leader of the state.

Thinking & Writing

What do you think is the most important rule in your community? Why? Write your answer here.

_____

_____

_____

_____

Unit 5

Living Together in Neighborhoods

People in one neighborhood may have come from other cities, states, and countries around the world.

- How are these neighbors alike?
- How are they different?
- How do they share special times together?

Unit Project

Learn about special days people honor and how they honor them. Think about this as you read Unit 5.

CHAPTER 11 Neighbors Are Alike and Different

Do you know where your neighbors are from? Many were born in the United States. Some came from other places in the world to live in your community.

Look at the picture of the people who live in this neighborhood. They all live in the United States now. Do they have the same color hair or skin?

▶ **What is one way these neighbors are alike? What is one way these neighbors are different? Write your answers here.**

_____

_____

_____

_____

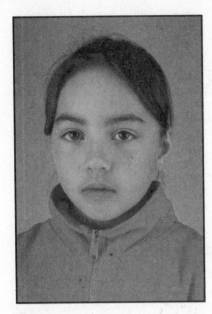

Rosa

Look at the map below and on page 105. This is a map of the world. Can you find the United States on the map?

➤ **Draw a green circle around the United States.**

Rosa's family comes from Mexico. They speak Spanish and English at home. Her family cooks many foods from Mexico.

➤ **Draw a line under the name of Mexico on the map.**

Put a C on the continent that is south of Mexico.

SOME COUNTRIES OF THE WORLD

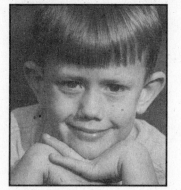

Jacob

Wesley

Jacob Corrigan's grandparents came from France.

➤ **Find France on the map. Draw a purple circle around it.**

Wesley Wong's family came from China. They speak Chinese. A special day for Wesley's family is Chinese New Year.

➤ **Find China on the map. Draw a blue circle around it.**

What ocean is east of China? Write your answer here.

_____

- - - - - - - - - - - - - - - - - - - -

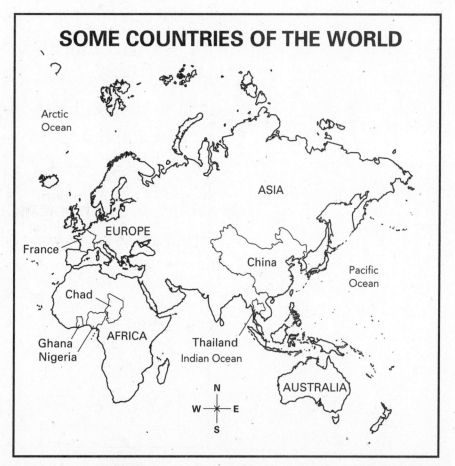

SOME COUNTRIES OF THE WORLD

Arctic Ocean

ASIA

EUROPE

France

China

Pacific Ocean

Chad

AFRICA

Thailand

Ghana
Nigeria

Indian Ocean

AUSTRALIA

N
W   E
S

People from other countries help make the United States special. They bring their own ways of doing things. They fix many of the same foods here. They still enjoy special days. They share these special things with their new neighbors in the United States.

Many people in this neighborhood speak Spanish. Every year they have a fiesta. A fiesta is a party for the neighborhood. The people eat Mexican foods. They sing Mexican songs. Some neighbors are not from Mexico. They learn about these special things at the fiesta.

➤ **What would you like to know about a fiesta? Write your question here.**

_____

_____

_____

Many people in this neighborhood are Chinese Americans. Look at the signs. Some are in English. Some are in Chinese.

➤ **How is this neighborhood like the one you live in? Write your answer here.**

_____

_____

_____

_____

Unit Project **Tip!**

Do you know any people from another country? Talk to them about their special days. Ask what they do on those days.

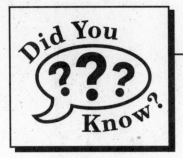

Did You ??? Know?

Becoming a Citizen

A **citizen** is a member of a country. People who move to the United States cannot be citizens right away. They must live here for a few years. They must learn to speak and read English. They must also learn about the United States.

After they have learned about the United States, people can become citizens. They must promise to be good citizens. They must promise to follow the laws of the United States.

➤ **What do you think a new citizen should know about the United States? Write your answer here.**

_____

- -

_____

Chapter Activity

Using a United States Map

People come to live in the United States from all over the world. Look at the map. Read each sentence. Do what it tells you.

1. Maria's family is from Peru. They live in Colorado. Put a ✔ on Colorado.

2. Shen's family is from China. They live in Kansas. Circle Kansas.

3. Shona's family is from Ghana. They live in Pennsylvania. Draw a line under Pennsylvania.

4. Andre's family is from France. They live in Louisiana. Put an **X** on Louisiana.

Name _____   Date _____

Finding Places on a World Map

Many people who live in the United States came from other countries. Look at the map of the world. Read each sentence. Do what it tells you.

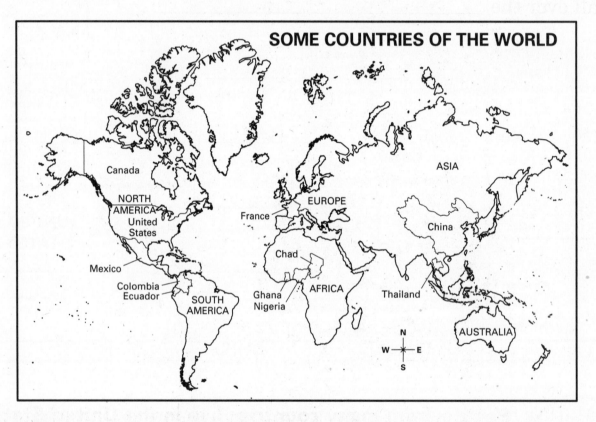

SOME COUNTRIES OF THE WORLD

1. Carlos came to the United States from Ecuador. People in Ecuador speak Spanish. Circle Ecuador in red on the map.

2. Lawan lives in Thailand. Her name means "pretty girl." Find Thailand on the map. Circle Thailand in blue.

3. Marie and her family moved to the United States from Ghana. Draw a line from Ghana to the United States.

Chapter Checkup ✓

➤ **Read each sentence. Find the word in the Word Box to finish each sentence. Write the word on the line.**

1. People come to live in the United States from

   _____

   all over the _____ .

2. People bring their way of doing things when

   _____

   they move to a new _____ .

3. People from other countries share their special ways of doing

   _____

   things with their new _____ .

   _____

4. A member of a country is a _____ .

Thinking & Writing

People from many countries live in the United States. How does this make our country better? Write your answer here.

_____

_____

_____

_____

CHAPTER 12 Neighbors Celebrate Together

Have you ever watched a parade? What kind of parade was it? Many communities have a parade to **celebrate** a special day. To celebrate is to honor. People in a town come to watch or take part in the parade. Many communities have parades on the Fourth of July, Columbus Day, and St. Patrick's Day.

➤ **Think about a parade you have seen. What did you like about it? Draw a picture here of the part you liked best.**

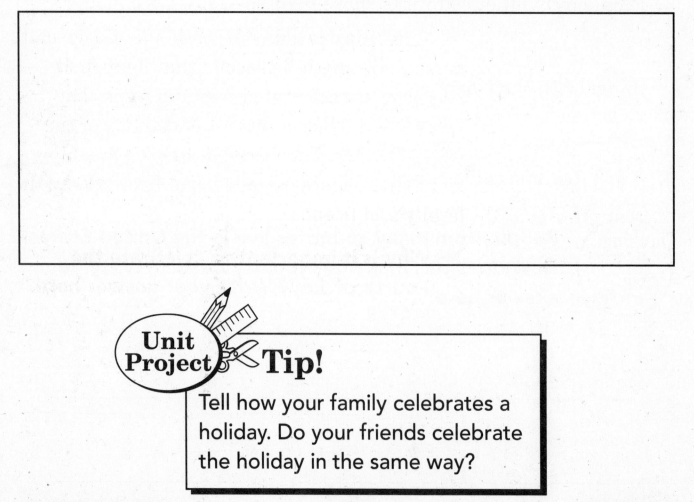

Unit Project **Tip!**

Tell how your family celebrates a holiday. Do your friends celebrate the holiday in the same way?

A **holiday** is a day to think about a special
person or something special that happened.
Holidays are celebrated in many ways. The
Fourth of July celebrates the birthday of the
United States. People celebrate this holiday
by having picnics, parades, and fireworks with
family and friends.

➤ **Why is it important to celebrate the
Fourth of July? Write your answer here.**

_____

_ _

_____

Look at the **time line** on these two pages. A time line shows a number of months or years in order. The marks on the time line stand for things that happened during those times. This time line shows the 12 months of the year. It shows when some of the holidays happen. The time line is like a picture of the year.

➤ **Which month comes after January? Write your answer here.**

_____

_____

Which month has two holidays? Write your answer here.

_____

_____

New Year's Day

Martin Luther King, Jr. Day   Memorial Day

Valentine's Day

January	February	March	April	May	June

➤ **Which holiday is in November? Write your answer here.**

_____

- -

_____

Find Memorial Day on the time line. Circle it.

When is your birthday? Find the month. Add your birthday to the time line.

Think of one more holiday that your family celebrates. Add the holiday to the time line.

Fourth of July   Labor Day

Thanksgiving

July	August	September	October	November	December

Celebrating Holidays

People around the world celebrate holidays. They celebrate some of the same days you do. But people in other countries also celebrate in their own special ways.

New Year's Day is a holiday in the United States. We celebrate by having parties. We also have big parades. Children in Belgium write notes on paper they have decorated. The children read the notes to their families on New Year's Day. Many Chinese people celebrate their New Year for four days.

➤ **Look at the pictures. How are these people celebrating their holidays? Write your answer here.**

_____

- -

_____

Chapter Activity

Reading a Chart

Remember that a chart puts facts in order. Look at the chart below to answer the questions.

Facts About Holidays			
Holiday	**When**	**Country**	**What People Do on the Holiday**
Kwanzaa	December 26 to January 1	United States	African Americans give gifts and light candles. They think about life in Africa.
St. Patrick's Day	March 17	Ireland	People go to church, enjoy family and community celebrations, and wear shamrocks.
Queen's Day	April 30	Netherlands	People honor the queen's birthday with parades, games, and fairs.

1. When do people celebrate St. Patrick's Day?

_____

- -

_____

2. Circle the name of the country on the chart that celebrates Queen's Day.

3. On what holiday do people think about life in Africa?

_____

- -

_____

4. On what holiday do people wear shamrocks?

_____

- -

_____

Chapter Checkup ✓

➤ **Read each sentence. Write T on the line if the sentence is true. Write F if it is false.**

_____ **1.** A holiday is a day to celebrate a person or something special that happened.

_____ **2.** We celebrate all holidays the same way.

_____ **3.** On the Fourth of July, we celebrate the birthday of the United States.

_____ **4.** You can use a time line to find out when things happened.

Think about the holiday you like best. Why is it important to celebrate this holiday? Write your answer here.

_____

_____

_____

_____

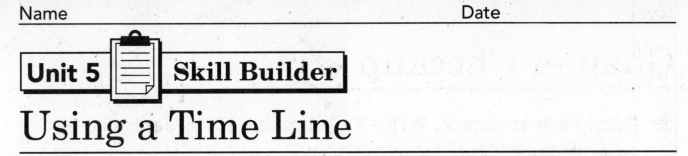

Unit 5 | Skill Builder

Using a Time Line

Remember that a time line shows when things happen. This time line shows when some celebrations happen in different parts of the United States. Look at the time line. Then answer the questions.

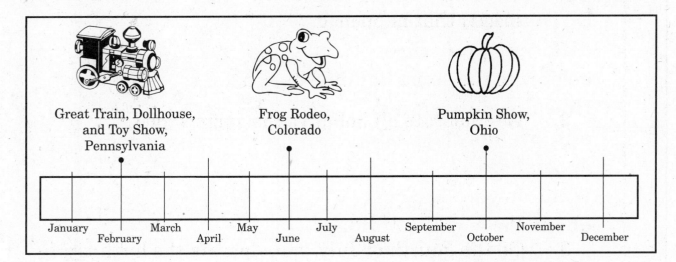

Great Train, Dollhouse, and Toy Show, Pennsylvania

Frog Rodeo, Colorado

Pumpkin Show, Ohio

January   February   March   April   May   June   July   August   September   October   November   December

1. At which celebration would you see lots of pumpkins?

_____

- -

_____

2. Where is the Great Train, Dollhouse, and Toy Show?

_____

- -

_____

3. During what month is the Frog Rodeo?

_____

- -

_____

Present Your Project

Now it's time to finish your project. Think about what you learned about the holidays people in our country celebrate. Think about answers to these questions.

- **Do Americans from different countries celebrate the same holidays?**
- **How do your family and friends celebrate special days?**
- **What do you like best about the way the holidays are celebrated?**

Now decide how you will present your project. Use one of these ideas or one of your own ideas.

- Make a poster to show how people celebrate holidays.
- Draw pictures to show how people celebrate. Put your drawings together in a booklet.
- Prepare a special news story about how people celebrate in different ways. Present your news report to your friends or family.
- Make a poster that tells people about a celebration that is coming soon. On your poster tell people the date of the celebration. Also tell how people will celebrate.

Unit 5 ✏️ Test

➤ **Read each sentence. Write T on the line if the sentence is true. Write F if it is false.**

_____ 1. People in the United States are all alike.

_____ 2. The United States is on the continent of North America.

_____ 3. People become citizens of the United States as soon as they move here.

_____ 4. People all around the world celebrate holidays.

When people move to the United States, they bring their ways of doing things with them. Why do you think they keep doing some things the same way? Write your answer here.

_____

_____

_____

_____

_____

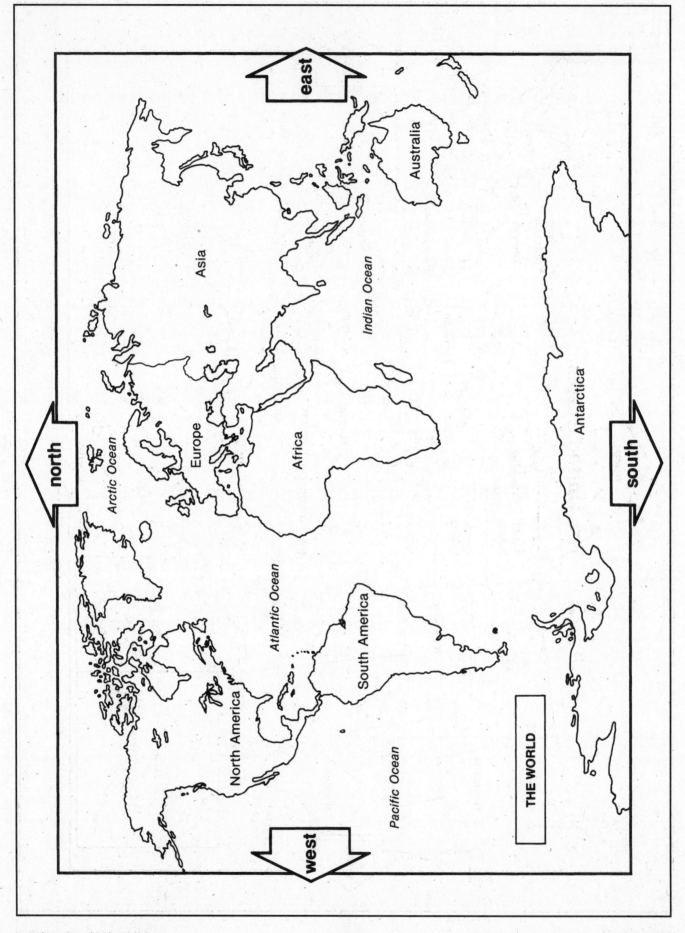

THE WORLD

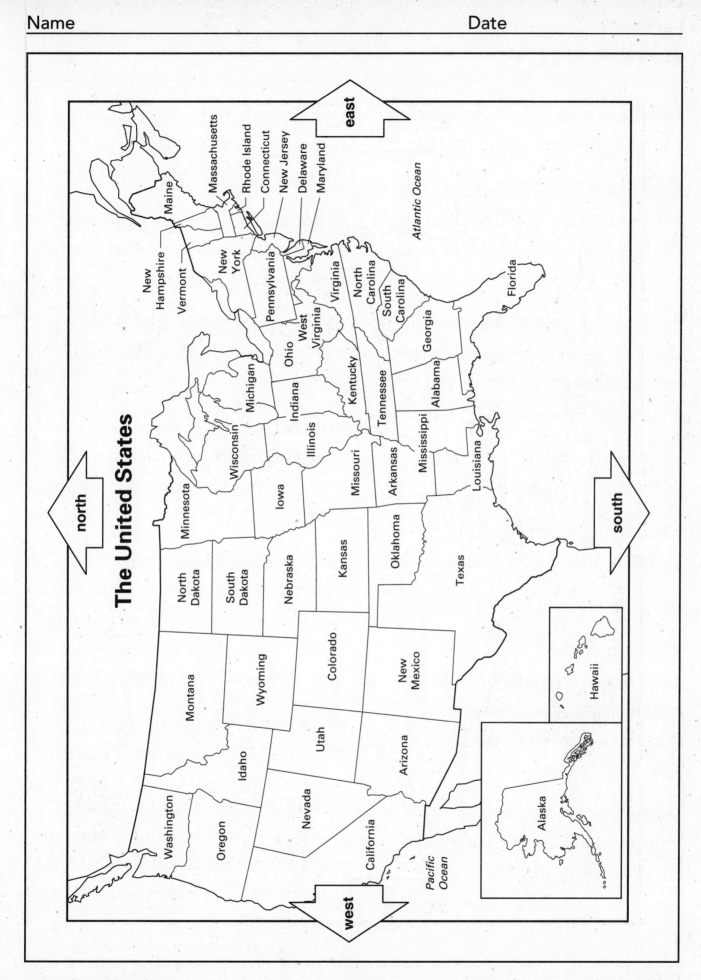

The United States

north

east

south

west

Massachusetts
Rhode Island
Connecticut
New Jersey
Delaware
Maryland

Maine
New Hampshire
Vermont
New York
Pennsylvania
West Virginia
Virginia
North Carolina
South Carolina
Georgia
Florida

Ohio
Michigan
Indiana
Illinois
Kentucky
Tennessee
Alabama
Mississippi
Louisiana

Wisconsin
Iowa
Missouri
Arkansas

Minnesota
North Dakota
South Dakota
Nebraska
Kansas
Oklahoma
Texas

Montana
Wyoming
Colorado
New Mexico

Idaho
Utah
Arizona

Washington
Oregon
Nevada
California

Atlantic Ocean

Pacific Ocean

Hawaii

Alaska

United States Map
Core Skills Social Studies 2, SV 9781419034244

Glossary

budget (page 62) A budget is a plan for how to spend money.

buffalo (page 27) Buffalo are large animals that lived on the plains. Some American Indians hunted buffalo.

capital (page 86) The capital is the city where the government meets. The governor works in the state capital.

celebrate (page 112) To celebrate is to honor.

chart (page 29) A chart puts facts in order.

citizen (page 108) A citizen is a member of a country.

community (page 46) A community is a town or city where people live, work, and play.

compass rose (page 9) A compass rose helps you find directions on a map.

continent (page 33) A continent is a very large area of land. There are seven continents.

directions (page 9) The four directions are north, south, east, and west.

globe (page 34) A globe is a model of Earth. It is round like a ball.

goods (page 46) Goods are things that people need and want. Some workers make goods for people to buy.

government (page 82) The government is those people who make the laws and see that the laws are obeyed. The government is made up of community leaders.

governor (page 85) The governor is the leader of a state.

holiday (page 113) A holiday is a day to think about a special person or something special that happened. The Fourth of July is a holiday.

income (page 61)   Income is the money people get for doing a job. People use their income to buy the things they need and want.

inset (page 84)   An inset is a box on a map. An inset may show something that is too far away to be seen on the map.

invention (page 16)   An invention is something that is made for the first time.

law (page 77)   A law is a rule for a community, state, or country. Laws help keep things fair for everyone.

leader (page 82)   A leader is a person who leads or is in charge.

map (page 8)   A map is a drawing of a place.

map key (page 8)   A map key shows or tells what the pictures on a map mean.

mayor (page 83)   The mayor is an important leader of a community. The mayor helps make laws in a city or town.

mountain (page 10)   A mountain is very high land.

need (page 45)   A need is something a person must have to live. Food, clothes, and a place to live are needs that all people have.

neighbor (page 6)   A neighbor is someone who lives near you.

neighborhood (page 6)   A neighborhood is a place to live, work, and play.

ocean (page 10)   An ocean is a very large body of salt water.

picture graph (page 45)   A picture graph uses pictures to show facts.

plain (page 11)   A plain is land that is flat. It is a good place to farm.

pollution (page 95)   Pollution is dirt, smoke, or trash. Pollution makes the air, water, and land dirty.

President (page 85)   The President is the leader of the United States.

river (page 11)   A river is a long stream of water that flows across land.

rule (page 75)   A rule tells us what to do or what not to do.

savings (page 64)   Savings is money that people keep for later.

service (page 48)   A service is a job someone does to help other people.

slave (page 58)   A slave is a person who is forced to work without pay.

state (page 84)   There are 50 states in the United States. Each state is made up of many communities.

taxes (page 65)   Money that people pay to the community where they live is called taxes. Taxes help pay for things like building roads and schools.

time line (page 114)   A time line shows things that happened during a certain amount of time.

volunteer (page 58)   A volunteer is a person who chooses to work without pay.

vote (page 83)   A vote is a choice. People of a community vote for their leaders. Each person gets to pick one person for each job.

want (page 45)   A want is something a person would like to have but can live without. Toys, trips, and pets are things that some people would like to have.

Answer Key

NOTE: For answers not provided, check that students have given an appropriate response and/or followed the directions given.

Page 8 library

Page 10 Students should place an **X** above the picture on the right of the mountain neighborhood. They should respond that warm clothes are needed in the mountains because it is cold.

Page 13
1. Students should circle the compass rose.
2. Students should color the library brown.
3. Students should color the house blue.
4. James Street

Page 14
1. plains   2. mountains
3. compass rose   4. map key
Answers will vary. Accept all reasonable answers.

Page 20
Students should number the picture on the left **1** and the picture on the right **2**.
3. There are more tall buildings and fewer trees. There are cars and buses instead of horses and carts.

Page 21
1. T   2. F   3. T   4. T   5. F
Answers will vary.

Page 24
1. F   2. T   3. T   4. T   5. F
Answers will vary. Accept all reasonable answers.

Page 29 American Indians built or made their homes. They made all their clothing.

Page 31
1. The Cree Indians
2. They were large, long, and made of wood.
3. Wood from trees; they built fires in their homes.

Page 32
1. were the first Americans.
2. hunting and farming.
3. clothing.
4. wrote with pictures instead of letters.
Answers will vary. Accept all reasonable answers.

Page 37 Students should answer that Jamestown had houses, gardens, and places for people to work, just like neighborhoods today.

Page 39
1. west
2. Pacific Ocean
3. South America

Page 40
1. Earth   2. continent
3. Atlantic   4. Thanksgiving
Answers will vary. Accept all reasonable answers.

Page 41
1. Atlantic Ocean
2. Students should put an **X** on Mexico.
3. Students should put a **C** on Europe.

Page 43
1. American Indians.
2. by making it.
3. Europe.
Answers will vary. Accept all reasonable answers.

Page 48
Photograph 1: help sick people; keep people well
Photograph 2: put out fires; save people

Page 50 Ice cream must be moved in a special truck. The ice cream must be kept cold so it will not melt.

Page 52
1. Students should circle Job City Community Workers
2. four
3. seven
4. Students should draw five postage stamps in the mail carrier row of the graph.

Page 53
1. community   2. needs   3. goods   4. service
The workers pictured give us services.

Page 56
Photograph **1.** unloading fish
Photograph **2.** moving snow

Page 59 Students should put a check under Services for teacher and dentist. They should put a check under Goods for farmer, worker in a shoe factory, and baker.

Page 60
1. F   2. T   3. T   4. T
Answers will vary. Accept all reasonable answers.

Page 61 Students should write **N** on the man grocery shopping and **W** on the woman buying jewelry.

Page 62
Students should put an **X** next to: How much will the trip cost? How much income do we have?

Page 63 Answers will vary, but student choices should not total more than $5.00.

Answer Key
Core Skills Social Studies 2, SV 9781419034244

Page 65 Students should respond that the teacher helps them learn, the police officer keeps them safe, and the librarian helps them find books or other library resources.

Page 68 Students should write *bowl of soup*, *shoes*, *house*, and *coat* under Needs and *TV*, *balloon*, and *computer* under Wants.

Page 69 Students should complete the chart by writing $1 in the column next to George Washington, $10 in the column next to Alexander Hamilton, and Andrew Jackson in the last column.

Page 70
1. to help them plan how to spend their money
2. to buy things we want that cost a lot of money
3. They use the money they get from taxes.
Answers will vary. Accept all reasonable answers.

Page 71
1. six judges   2. four school bus drivers
3. Students should draw six trees in the city park workers row of the graph.
4. Answers will vary. Accept all reasonable answers.

Page 73
1. income   2. wants   3. slaves   4. services
Answers will vary. Accept all reasonable answers.

Page 77 how fast they can go

Page 78
Students should put a **1** in the box next to the picture of the police officer stopping traffic, a **2** in the box next to the children walking dogs, and a **3** in the box next to the girl littering in the park. They should also put a check mark next to the picture of the girl littering.

Page 80 Students should correctly match the pictures with the rules.

Page 81
1. Rules and laws help people live together.
2. Obey all traffic laws.
3. to keep people safe
Answers will vary. Accept all reasonable answers.

Page 88
1. Students should color Canada green.
2. Students should circle Ottawa; Washington, D.C.; and Mexico City.
3. Washington, D.C.
4. Students should color Mexico brown.

Page 89
1. National capital
2. Students should mark an **X** on their state. They should mark an **O** on a state north or south of their state.
3. east

Page 90
1. leaders   2. vote   3. governor   4. President
Answers will vary. Accept all reasonable answers.

Page 92 The grass must be cut; the trash must be picked up. The field needs to be cleaned.

Page 93 Students should circle digging, picking up cans, and raking the grass.

Page 97
1. panther
2. whale and sea turtle
3. Students should put a T on Asia.
4. Students should put a B in North America.

Page 98
1. F   2. T   3. T   4. F
Answers will vary. Accept all reasonable answers.

Page 99
1. Students should circle Washington, D.C.
2. Students should color three states on the East coast red.
3. Students should color three states next to the Pacific Ocean blue.
4. Students should put an **N** on the north part of Alaska.

Page 101
1. vote   2. laws   3. pollution   4. governor
Answers will vary. Accept all reasonable answers.

Page 105 Pacific Ocean

Page 111
1. world   2. country   3. neighbors   4. citizen
Answers will vary. Accept all responsible answers.

Page 114 February comes right after January. January has two holidays.

Page 115 Thanksgiving

Page 117
1. March 17
2. Students should circle the Netherlands on the chart.
3. Kwanzaa
4. St. Patrick's Day

Page 118
1. T   2. F   3. T   4. T
Answers will vary. Accept all reasonable answers.

Page 119
1. Pumpkin Show
2. Pennsylvania
3. June

Page 121
1. F   2. T   3. F   4. T
Answers will vary. Accept all reasonable answers.